There Is a Tomorrow
My Life

by

Burgel Mertens

To my dear friend Eugen
with Love *Burgel*

Oct. 2nd, 2009

Ps. 32:8 "I will watch over you
with my eye upon you "

(see bookcover)

DORRANCE PUBLISHING CO., INC.
PITTSBURGH, PENNSYLVANIA 15222

ISBN: 978-1-4349-0205-4
Library of Congress Control Number: 2009921844

Printed in the United States of America

First Printing

For information or to order additional books, please write:
Dorrance Publishing Co., Inc.
701 Smithfield St.
Pittsburgh, Pennsylvania 15222
U.S.A.
1-800-788-7654
www.dorrancebookstore.com

Dedication

In thankfulness to the Lord, who inspired me to write this book. With love to my daughter, Sylvia; son, Robby; all my grandchildren and great-grandchildren; and especially my great-granddaughter, Pumuckl, who brought so much joy in our life. Also, to my sister, Heidi, who took care of us, especially of my husband, when we needed help.

As a Little Child: WWII

I remember WWII. When the war began in 1939, I was six years old. My little sister was born in 1941; my father did not join the army from the beginning in 1939. He was forced to join the army after that. I don't know the exact date or year. After the war was over in 1945, the Russians took over the power of the leadership over East Germany. From that time, the communism was the regime under the Russian, and this brought the terrible time of starving and captivation of East –Germany, which I will explain later in my book. When I was a little child we had to cover all the windows with blankets and dark materials so the English airplanes, who were then our enemies, could not see any lights when flying over our village. The police checked every evening from house to house to make sure no lights were shining through the windows. People really got in trouble if they were careless and did not follow the instructions.

For me it did not really matter, because I was too young to understand the danger, but when the sirens went on to give the alarm warning that the bombers were on the way to fly over our village, everyone rushed into the basement, which was used as a bunker. They all were so quiet and still. I saw the fear in each face, and when a bomb fell nearby and destroyed houses, and in many cases a whole city, I heard babies and mothers crying. I saw also that mothers were praying, although no religious people were accepted then. Everybody was so scared and frightened that the next bomb could hit their house.

When, after some hours, the sirens went on again, telling us the danger was over and we were allowed to go back in our home, we were so relieved. But even when we were allowed to go back in our home, turning on lights was still prohibited; only candles were allowed. As a little child I found it often romantic, not realizing how frustrating it was for others. I thought, when my mother was around me, nothing could ever harm me.

Bombarding the City of Dresden (Sachsen)

The worst experience my family and I had was when Dresden was attacked. Dresden (Sachsen) had a population of approximately 500,000, and with the third bombardment over Dresden in 1945, Dresden's Jewish population was virtually wiped out. Dresden was not far from our village, and we felt the earth shaking and the entire sky was red and purple from the fire which destroyed that big city. All those beautiful buildings—museums, theatres, cathedrals, universities, etc.—were totally gone. Only ashes were left. That brought not only the people of Dresden to their knees, but whole Sachsen and Ergebirge mourned over this unbelievable tragedy.

Two other neighbour-cities, Annaberg and Chemnitz, very close to our village of Cranzahl where I lived, were bombarded and destroyed. I will never forget the loud noises from the crashes I heard, and I know nobody else will. It sounded like it was happening right next to us. People were crying, and what was so comforting—they prayed! Yes, the Lord had mercy on us and saved our house from all these disasters.

My mother was an emergency Red Cross nurse and was called often in the middle of the night to the train station, because wounded German soldiers arrived and needed help right away. Many of them lost their arms or legs, and many of them died in my mother's arms.

Every time a new transport arrived, my mother searched all the wagons hoping to find my father, but he was never among them. Since we did not hear anything from him we did not know if he was dead or only captured in a Russian camp. I can't imagine what my poor mother went through to be strong for her five children.

Postcard Addressed to My Father Arrived

One day a postcard from a comrade of my father arrived, saying, "Hi, Oskar, I hope you made it home safe. Let me hear from you. Your comrade!"

Because of this note my mother and older brother (who took over many responsibilities while my father was in the war) got new hope our father was alive. My mother wrote back asking him to let her know more about her husband.

I remember as a young child how kind my father was. In my imagination I saw my father in every man I met on the street. I believed with all my heart that my father would come home and I would see him again.

An Angel Appeared to Me

One night while my mother was called to the wounded soldiers' transport, I did not feel well. I went to my grandma's house, hoping I could sleep there. My grandma let me sleep on a sofa in her living room. In the middle of the night I saw an angel in the corner beside the door. She wore a white dress and had white wings. I could not see her face clearly, but she spoke to me and said: *"Do not be afraid and sad; your father will be saved and home."*

The next day I was so excited when I told my mother and brother about it. They did not believe me, especially my brother.

I have to tell you, when I was a baby my mother said I was very different from other babies. I cried as soon as somebody looked in my bed or carriage who was evil. Even when my mother had a visitor who was not a good person, I cried. They figured out that I was able to foresee things, what would happen in the future. Many times my mother experienced that I sensed things which really occurred later.

My mother believed in me, that I was gifted to sense things and that I could feel the difference between good and evil people, but my brother made fun of me and did not believe any of these things. I was very sensitive about that but was relieved that some close friends of my mother knew my abilities and paid attention to what I could foresee. They experienced some incidents I did prophesy and which therefore could be prevented.

So I was waiting for the things what the angel told me would happen. I waited and waited, but my father did not show up. I heard my brother and some others saying, "It was her imagination again." That hurt. I believed so strongly that the message the angel gave me was not my imagination and had a meaning.

The Angel Said My Father Is Safe and Home!

My mother was still waiting to hear from her husband's comrade who had written the postcard addressed to my father and to whom she had written back. She wanted to know more about what was going on. One day he suddenly stood before my mother, and he was so shocked and disappointed not to see my father. When my mother told him that my father had never made it home, he was so sad.

He told us they had escaped together from a Russian prison and later went separate ways to get home. The war was already over (1945), but soldiers were missing and no one knew if they were still alive, dead, or being held in a Russian or Czechoslovakian prison. He gave the exact date and time when they separated and when my father fled over Cech-Slovanian (Tschechoslowakei) because it was the shortest way to our home for my father.

When we heard the day and time we realized that was the exact day and time when three soldiers were hanged on trees. It was only fifty kilometers away from our home. We knew in our hearts one of them was my father. It is not describable what everyone went through, especially my mother. How lucky my mother was when neighbours or farmers gave her some potato skins, from which she made a meal. Sometimes if she was lucky, she got a whole potato, which she grinded in a pot of water and made into soup. We all thought it was delicious.

But for me it came back in my mind what the angel said that my father is saved and will be home. I was right away convinced that this was an important message from the angel. It was such a relief for me, because I knew the angel wanted me to know that my father gave his heart to Jesus before he died, and therefore he is *saved* and *home*, home with Jesus.

This statement was a closure for me and my mother; it set us, finally, free from all the grief and uncertainty we carried.

Thank you, Lord!

Surviving Communism after WWII

Fears and Tears

I was a thirteen-year old girl living in a small town when the Russians took over after WWII. As I mentioned earlier, my father did not come back from the war and my mother tried so hard to survive with her five children. We were starving and begging for food for so many years.

I remember in school, I did homework for other classmates who were more fortunate then me and still had a father or were living on a farm in exchange to get their sandwiches or any other food.

I was really gifted at imitating other people. My teacher was a funny-looking man and had strange behaviors. I was often asked to copy him before the class; they offered me a sandwich for doing it. I did and my classmates couldn't hide their laughing when he entered the classroom. There were times when I had no time to get back to my place and hid behind his desk. As a penalty sometimes I had to write many pages from *Die Glocke,* by Schiller. It had to be in handwriting, which was not a big punishment for me because I loved writing anyway.

When my teacher came in our classroom, he first hung up his coat on a rack beside his desk, and then he put his scarf very carefully over the coat, took his black hat off, and put it the same strange way above the rack. When he talked he put his mouth in a funny position and crossed one hand over the other and tipped with his fingers on his desk. It was so easy for me to mimic him, and I looked forward to getting the reward in the form of food from my classmates. You can image how much fun my classmates had to see me acting the way our teacher did. I am not ashamed of using this gift to survive, but later I felt sorry for my teacher, for impersonating him and giving him a hard time.

I have to let you know that my family survived only on some potato peels, which we often got from people who were more fortunate then we and sometimes put leftovers in the garbage. My oldest brother, who took over most of the responsibilities of my father when he was home, worried with my mom about not getting the help for us we needed. He was strong and, for his young age, very mature and a blessing to his siblings and our mom. But for me, I could not take it anymore. I cried in my sleep thinking all the time how could I change this life. I was always trying to find a solution to escape from this terrible life. My mind was occupied day and night.

From my early childhood on, I wanted so badly to have a better life. I wanted to see what was out there in the world. I dreamed about finding a chance to change things for myself in this world. As young as I was, I also was strong enough to believe I would be able to change my situation. I thought it was so unfair that I had to starve and live in such poor conditions. Every day I was searching for a solution as to how I could escape from the life I was unwillingly forced into.

I found out I had an older cousin from my father's side living in Weferlingen near the border to West Germany, where the Americans took over after the war. My mind was working over-time. We all knew the people in West Germany had enough food and nobody had to starve. I longed to be in West Germany, where my older sister had managed to escape some years ago, before escaping became so hard. How could I do the same thing without being caught? I could not sleep for thinking all the time what to do.

My whole life, I never gave up and always found a way to make my life more bearable. I wanted a better life, but to escape from East Germany to West Germany was almost impossible; there was a minefield between the Russian and American Zone one had to cross.

But to have a better life, you have to take the risk and forget all the danger—like what could happen when you step on a mine. I thought, what difference would it make to starve to death or to step on a mine and die there. At least I did my best trying to change my terrible life. I was always thinking about my mom, what it would bring to her if something happened to me, but I also had in my mind that if I were successful, it could not only change my life for the better but my family's too.

I will never forget what our family had to go through to survive. Our bodies were covered with hunger boils and serious infection so that every part of our bodies was hurting. My mother's body was the worst, because when we had some food she gave it to her children. She did everything in her power to save us from not having enough food to survive. We had a great mother, and we loved her so much. She was very strong, and with the help of my oldest brother she did everything in her power, to raise her children to be strong too. Giving her children all the food she had without thinking of herself was certainly the reason why her body was the most infected. I will also never forget hearing my mother crying in the night. I knew she was thinking of her children and how she could help us, but she saw no way to do that.

One night, unable to sleep, I decided to visit my cousin and his family in Weferlingen, only ten minutes away from the border between Weferlingen (East Germany) and Oebisfelde (West Germany). I was hoping they would welcome me and I could stay there for a while.

I stayed at his house for seven days, thinking day and night how could I possibly escape from there to the other side. On the eighth day I got up early and took a small plastic bag with some personal things. I had to do these preparations very secretly, because everyone knew if people tried to escape or even said things against the communism, they were put away and you never heard of them again. I tell you that so you can better understand the scary situation in which I was. I was aware of that, but I had to take that risk.

On the eighth day I went close to the border and saw all the many Russian soldiers with rifles on their shoulders standing and walking around; I got really frightened. I was so discouraged and did not know what I should do. Should I go home to the life I hated so much, or should I not give up and figure out what possibilities were there? I decided not to give up.

The Day I Tried Passing the Minefield to Escape

I was watching the whole day what was going on there and what would be my chance to escape successfully. Nothing really was encouraging since I saw the Russians all over the place. I spied the whole day and found out the time when the patrol shifts changed.

The best time to try to flee was supposedly during the night. I had no money, I had no food—and was hungry! The sandwich I brought with me I had already ate in the morning.

The dark started coming, and shortly before midnight I thought it was the perfect time to risk my escape. Maybe I was lucky, because everyone was sleeping. The shift change would not be earlier then the next day in the morning.

I stepped on the minefield and got only ten or twenty meters when I heard a loud voice: "Stoy," which means stop. I right away stood still and did what you do in such situations—you pray! I saw my mom very often on her knees praying; she must have had many of these terrible moments. I certainly found myself right there in serious trouble and was only relying on the Lord's help.

I was crying and praying and my whole body were shaking. The soldier brought me to a small house and put me in the basement, where at least twelve other people already were. I will continue to talk about what happened to me then later in this book.

All my life my mother told me, "God is always with you. Only He is able to change unhappy situations like that, if you confide and trust in Him." I trusted him with all my heart! I also knew that Jesus wanted his children to come to Him, so I did; I am his child.

I have to go back a little to when I attended a school where everyone had to hide believing in the Lord Jesus Christ. Going to a church was not appreciated, and people who did go and did not honor this command were often picked up from home, and were never again seen, so I understand why my mother never allowed us to go to a church or any home meetings.

Caught and Put in a Basement Prison

Back to the night when a Russian soldier stopped me to cross the minefield and brought me to the dark basement where already twelve other adults were captured.

There were no windows and no toilets. Everybody was sitting on a water pail, which they also had to use as a toilet. This was really scary, and I started crying and quietly praying, afraid someone would figure out what I was doing. I cried out to my Father and Lord Jesus Christ to help me.

One mature woman showed me compassion and had tears in her eyes too. Most of them could not understand why a young girl like me was put in this dark prison-like room. I was so hungry, and I had to go to the toilet so badly. I was in such pain, and I cried louder and louder. The nice woman knocked on the door and screamed, "Help, Help!"

Finally a soldier opened the door. It was not the same one who put me in the basement, and when he looked at me he let me go to a toilet upstairs and even gave me some bread and bacon to eat.

He asked me all these questions but acted very friendly. I was so scared, because I had heard all about the terrible things soldiers were doing to women. I was very skinny and undeveloped as a result of the lack of nourishment. Then he told me he remembered his child, who must be my age. I knew then I was in good hands and my fears were gone. He let me rest for a while, and then he set me free and let me go home. He said in fatherly voice, "Before the next shift at six A.M. arrives, you must be gone. Please don't come back and try again. The other soldiers might not be so merciful and understanding."

I knew it was the Lord who heard my cry. When I came to my cousin's house they were wondering where I was. I could not tell them that I tried to escape; I would put them in jeopardy. I lied about being with a friend I met some days ago. They did not doubt me at all, and I was relieved.

That was really a scary experience, but did I learn from it?

Not even close. I was still in the same boat, still in East Germany. There had to be another way to escape to the other side, but how?

The question of how needed to be solved, but only by a miracle. Lord, please, let it happen. I am lost without Your help.

Waiting for a Miracle

I went back to my cousin's house, waiting for an opportunity, a window to open showing me a way to escape. I knew there must be another solution.

In return for staying in my cousin's house, I helped as much as I could in their household by looking after five small kids. They did not have much food either, but at least they had flour, milk, bread, butter, potatoes, and sometimes meat. Every night I prayed for a miracle to happen and for a door to open.

Three days later I met a young woman (two years older), and she told me that she worked in a sugar factory in Oebisfelde in West Germany. Every morning she was brought with twenty other workers by bus over the border to the other side. In the evening they came back the same way. Everyone had a special passport with their photos on it that they had to show to a Russian soldier when they passed the border. We talked and talked and looked for a way how I could get on that bus instead of her without being recognized. We discussed every little detail, and she was willing to help me.

The Lord was with me to bring that lady into my life. I can't thank Him enough that she was willing to risk giving me her passport. I asked her to pray for me, and she said yes and that "everything will be fine."

On Monday morning I went to where the bus was waiting, got in, and was sitting exactly where my friend told me to. The lady beside me knew already that I was the one who had to give her the passport after we were on the other side. When we got close to the border, I was so nervous, and I thought everyone could see that. At the border the bus stopped and a Russian soldier opened the door. Every passenger showed their passport by holding it up. The Russian officer looked them over briefly, said, "Okay," and closed the door. It was unreal for me that this could be over and done with and I would be in West Germany. When the bus stopped at the factory in Oebisfelde, all the workers got out, going to their jobs. Before the lady who was sitting beside me left, I gave her the passport of my friend and said thank you.

I was standing there all by myself, not knowing what I would do next. I could not see any soldiers around me, and that's when I realized I was free. An officer saw me standing there and wanted to know if he could help me. I told him I was a fugitive and didn't know what I had to do now. He was very helpful and brought me to a building where another officer questioned me about the reason why I escaped (even they knew what people in East Germany had to go through). They put me in a camp where I was examined for lice and other health issues. Best of all, they gave me good food.

When I was questioned about my plans and where I wanted to go, I told them I planned to find my sister and stay with her. I wanted to stay in West Germany, get a job to make a living, and maybe support my poor family at home. My heart was heavy when I thought about home and my little four-year-old sister there. It really broke my heart when I realized I had left her at home starving and suffering the things I went through, but I did not give up hope and strongly believed I could make a difference in my and my family's life. I did not know how, but I felt that the Lord was with me and already knew the answer. I put my trust in Him who comforted me that moment and gave me hope.

Since I had no address for my sister and knew only the city where she was living and was employed, the officers had to go through so much trouble to find her. When they finally found her address and contacted her, asking her to send money for a ticket to put her sister on a train to Luebeck, where she should pick me up, she said yes but acted so strange. I asked if I could talk to her myself, and when I did, I was disappointed. I could not figure out why she barely spoke and why she told me she was not sure I could stay with her. Later I found out why and found out, too, why she never stayed in contact with my family and did not support them.

I had to wait in that camp until the money for the ticket arrived. I was registered and a new passport was handed to me. You can't imagine how I felt. I was free and ready for a new future. I thought my life would change right away for the better. I was so full of hope and did not know that the real journey for a thirteen-year-old girl had just begun.

Lost at the Huge Train Station in Luebeck

When I arrived at that huge train Station, I could not see my sister. I looked in every direction. I saw so many people, but not my sister. I started crying and felt totally lost, because she told me she would be there. The moment a police officer wanted to help me, I saw my sister at the staircase looking for me. I ran to her. We held each other in our arms. Tears of happiness ran down our faces, and my sister said, "Come on, I will take you to my place."

She took me to the house where she was employed, which was huge and very nice. She gave me chocolate milk, buns, and butter to eat, which was for me like heaven. I will never in my life forget what I felt that moment. It was a dream came true.

My sister told me not to eat so hastily, otherwise I could get sick after starving so long. We had so much to talk about, life at home and our family. She was amazed by what I was risking to escape to West Germany at my young age.

I was not even there two hours with my sister when the phone rang. Her boss told her that he knew she had a visitor and he wanted her out right away. For us it was a mystery how could they know; we assumed the house was watched to see who was coming and going. When my sister explained that her little sister had come for a visit and wanted to stay with her for a while, they gave her an ultimatum. I could stay only one night and had to leave in the morning. She was so sad when she told me that. We talked the whole night but could not figure out why I had to leave. It did not make sense to us at all. There were questions over questions about where I should go.

The next morning my sister brought me to a nearby camp in Poeppendorf where I had to go through the same procedure I had to in the camp in Oebisfelde.

It still troubled me why I could not stay in that beautiful big house with my sister. I got the answer much later, but she told me how happy she was to get this job right away after she escaped from East Germany and did not think about why she had to sign the agreement not to talk to anyone about what and for whom she was working. The mail was censored, too, and you had to be careful what you wrote in letters.

Where Could I Go after Leaving My Sister's House?

When my sister left after she dropped me off at the camp, I was crying. It was a big camp and lots of fugitives who escaped from East Germany got support. They helped each of them to find a job somewhere. That was what they tried for me.

After staying in that camp for approximately three weeks, I was transferred to another camp in Nordrhein-Westfalen. There I had to stay until they found a job for me. I had to wait only two weeks. In the meantime I turned fourteen years old and was still full of hope for a better life. I was so excited about what my life would be and where they would find a job for me and what I would have to do. I was willing to do anything, but how little did I know how hard life can be.

A day before I was shipped to the other camp in Rheinland-Westfalen, my sister came to see me. It was a sad good-bye, and she promised to visit me very soon after she knew where I was. At least I had her phone number. I felt a little homeless and was hoping to find a good place with a nice family.

In that camp I remember meeting a young boy, maybe my age or little older, and I experienced my first kiss. He broke a flower from a jasmine bush, gave it to me, and said: "This beautiful white flower will always remind me of your pure innocence and your beautiful smell." I have kept this little incident in my memory all these years. I even remember his name, Rudolf. I will always remember my first kiss.

No one can see in their future; therefore, you go by faith and make the best of every situation.

My First Job in Life at Age Fourteen

How exited I was to have my first job. One morning I was brought to a big chicken farm in Widdersdorf, a very small town near Rheinland. When I met my female boss I was so disappointed. She was not a friendly woman and her voice was cold and harsh. When she introduced to me all the duties she expected me to do, my heart was pounding with fear. How could I accomplish so many assignments without any experience? I had no education either, because I dropped out of school when I was thirteen to escape the terrible life I was living.

I encouraged myself to be strong and to do everything in my power to perform what I was asked to do.

It was so hard for me. My workday started 7:30 A.M., and there was never really an end. After supper I had to do the dishes, which took me often until nearly midnight. I got only three short breaks during the day. One for breakfast, one for lunchtime, and one for supper. My food for each week was rationed.

Every Saturday morning each of her servants (there were four including me) received one pound butter, one glass of jam, and one glass of syrup, which had to last for one week. At least bread, milk, and potatoes were available without asking. The pay was so low it covered only toilet utensils and some personal care. I had no hope to send food or money home to my family if I stayed at this place. That made me really frustrated, which never stopped me from searching for a way out. Crying in my bed was a regular thing. I felt so homesick and lost, but I was stuck there and saw no way to escape or to find another job. I had no opportunity to meet other people.

I prayed every night to the Lord, my only hope. Did the Lord hear my cry? I wanted to give up, because I did not feel His helping hand, and I started doubting that God even existed. I am sorry to tell you that, but I was to the point of giving up totally and not believing in the Lord anymore. Did the Lord give up on me? I found out later, He did not.

One day my boss had to go in the hospital for surgery. When I visited her, I met a friendly woman lying in a bed beside her. It felt so good to have somebody to talk to. She told me that her cook had suddenly quit for personal reasons and she was desperate to find a replacement.

You know by now how my mind was working. Did I see a chance?

I told her I would be pleased if she hired me, even though I was very young, and that I could cook. It was a lie. How in the world would I be able to cook for a family of six? But I had to take this opportunity; at least I had to try. This nice lady was so desperate that she hired me right there in the hospital without any questions. I did not realize that the Lord was working because I had stopped believing in Him. I am so ashamed that I did.

A few days later, when the lady was discharged from the hospital, she picked me up at my old workplace and took me to her house in Klein Koenigsdorf, on the Rhein River. It was a big house, and when she showed me the kitchen I was impressed how large and modernly equipped it was. I saw myself standing at that big stove with an extra oven to cook for so many people without any knowledge of how to do it. I was so afraid of what I had agreed to and was wondering what I had gotten into.

She was living with her husband, his brother, two young boys (one of them was mentally disabled). Sometimes two other men who worked in the field came for supper. There was also an older women who came each morning and evening as a milkmaid who was so helpful to me and helped me in many situations. I confided in her and she understood me.

New Challenge as a Cook

Every evening before the milk woman left for home we discussed the meal what was scheduled for the next day. She gave me instructions which I wrote on a piece of paper so I was able to prepare the meal on the next day. She helped me with so many things, and later I realized she must have been sent from heaven. Then she bought a cookbook for me, which I studied each night to be prepared to cook the meals required. The new boss lady saw my struggle, and how thankful I was that she realized how seriously I tried to satisfy her so as not to lose that job.

Again I was amazed by how I handled every situation and found help and solutions in my conflicts. I could ask that nice milk woman about anything and she never got tired of listening or helping me. My ambition to do a good job made me strong and even happy.

One day I got a letter from Rudolf, the boy I met in the camp in Rheinland-Westfalen. He searched for me and wanted to meet me. I did not write back; I was still very shy and scared of what could happened if we would meet again. That was the last time I heard from him, but I think each of us will always remember our first kiss.

I think it was even a miracle that everyone liked my cooking very much and only my boss and the milkmaid knew I was not experienced and had no idea how to cook. I saw her often smiling when I got compliments. The paycheck was satisfying, and on top of that I got such delicious food and I was able to send some groceries and a little money home. I did not realized then that all these opened windows came from the Lord. Yes, the Lord changed all bad experiences for the good and made everything possible.

One night while I lay in my bed I heard a cat outside at my window crying terribly. It frightened me so much because it sounded like my little four-year-old sister crying. Suddenly I got really homesick, and I asked my boss to give me a few weeks off to visit my family. It was shortly before Christmas. She asked her husband, who said yes, and the woman who milked the cows agreed to cook for them in the meantime. I phoned my sister, asking her to come home with me for the Christmas holidays. The next day she called back and said yes, she could. No one can imagine how I felt and how happy I was about having a good job, nice caring people around me, and now, for the first time after I escaped, to see my loving family. We assumed visiting home would not be so dangerous anymore.

We arranged the flights, each of us from different airports, to the destination, Hannover, where my sister and I met and from where we were picked up from relatives. It was a happy *Wiedersehen*. Both of us brought food, fruit, and chocolate along, because these things you could never buy in East Germany once the communistic regime took over after Germany lost the war.

My sister and I we were so overwhelmed with joy to bring all these goodies home to our family at Christmas time. I spent most of the time with my little sister whom I loved so much. Although it was strange for me that my mother and my sister were talking with each other almost till midnight. They carried a secret we did not know about, and they did not let anybody know. I was really jealous that they treated me like a little child when I felt grown up and had accomplished so many things that only adults were able to do, but I was happy to be home and united with my family, especially with my little sister.

When we unpacked all the good food and goodies and I saw my siblings and mother staring at these groceries they had never seen before, it felt like heaven on earth, and the first time in my life I felt like I could make a difference in my and my family's life. Was it really true?

I went to bed with my little sister in my arms and was more than happy.

Christmas 1949 with My Family in East Germany

It was the Christmas I had waited for for so long; I was finally reunited with my family again.

When I got up, with my little sister sleeping in my arms on Christmas Eve, I was surprised that all my family were already sitting at the breakfast table. There was so much to talk about, and the joy of being together was indescribable. The beautifully decorated Christmas tree was standing in the corner of our living room. Everything looked so familiar to me, because all the Christmas decorations were saved from one year to the other and I truly remembered all of them. Tears of joy were in everybody's eyes and our great love for each other filled our home. Happiness is a wonderful feeling, and I wanted so badly for this happiness to never go away.

Not one of us could know that this Christmas Eve would end with sadness because an unexpected surprise happened. Our joy would be gone and replaced with tears of sorrows.

I would like to tell you a little bit about the tradition in my homeland, *Erzgebirge*, on Christmas Eve. At exactly 6 P.M. supper was served in each household. The meals were the same in every family; there were nine original dishes prepared in each household. The important dish was potatoes, sauerkraut, and bratwurst. In the middle of the table was a candle and underneath was a penny. It symbolized that we would have enough money the next year. Beside the candleholder was a plate with one slice of bread and salt. That was the symbol of having enough daily bread and food. Another dish symbolized health, and we all had to eat a little bit from each of them. After my mother prayed, no one was allowed to get up while we had our meal. Only after my mother would say, "Thanks to the Lord," were we excused from the table.

It did not come to that, because in the middle of our supper (we were six people, my mother and five children) the doorbell rang. Holding on to our tradition, nobody wanted to get up to open the door. The doorbell did not stop ringing. We could not believe that someone would visit another family; for everyone living in *Erzgebirge* this was a holy time. Finally my brother decided to get up and opened the door.

We heard him saying, "Oh no, What is going on? Why are you here?" Two police officers were asking for my sister. They came in and took her with them. They did not tell us why she was arrested or where they took her. That was a very sad Christmas for all of us.

I was relieved that they did not ask about me because I had escaped from East Germany too.

We did not hear from her or the police about what happened to my sister. When my mother tried to see her at the police station, she was not there. I did not find out what took place because I had to fly back to my job. My holiday time was over and I had to return to West Germany. It was a sad good-bye because I had to leave with the uncertainty of where my sister might be. For me life had to go on, and I was so relieved that I was able to return without being arrested.

When I arrived in Klein Koenigsdorf in West Germany, my boss and all the others were so happy to see me and welcomed me with open arms. They told me how they missed me, but mostly my cooking. It made me really happy to hear that. My mother gave me a cookbook for Christmas. I appreciated this gift so much and could not wait to study all the recipes. I surprised my boss and her family every day with a new recipe and a new delicious meal. My enthusiasm and passion for cooking was so much appreciated that after a week I got a raise. My heart jumped for joy, because that enabled me to send more food home.

Some weeks went by and I did not hear anything from my sister and neither did my mother. We could only communicate by mail. Only privileged families were allowed to have phones in their houses. Our family was for sure not one of them, because my mother refused to join the Communist party, SED (Soialistische Einheitspartei Deutschland), and she did not follow the proclamation about hanging the communist flag out of our windows. That was unwise and risky behavior for my mother, for which she had to later pay a hurtful price.

I continued to send food weekly to my family's home. My parcels must be delivered and I assumed they received them, but I was wondering why I had not heard from anybody since I had come back from my holiday in East Germany. A whole month went by without my knowing what was going on. One day I could not believe my eyes; my sister suddenly stood before me asking if she could stay with me for a short time. When I asked my boss, who had become a good friend to me, she said yes and gave her a place to stay.

I was so happy to see her, but more anxious to hear what happened to her when she was arrested and why she came to the place I worked. I had so many questions and wanted explanations about all these secrets which were hidden for me.

We had so many sleepless nights because we were talking and talking. In the morning we were very tired, but my sister helped me with housekeeping and cooking, and therefore my employer and her family had no reason to be disappointed in my work.

After my sister stayed with us for a week, she had to look for a new employment and left. Now I knew the reason because she told me. After she was arrested and put in prison, she had to sign an agreement that she would spy for the Russians; otherwise they wouldn't let her go. She did not know what she was agreeing to, but she wanted to be free from all those questions and wanted so badly to go home. The moment she arrived at her employer's house in Luebeck in West Germany, she was fired without any explanation. But strange things appeared to her, because they knew all about the arrest and that she had been in a Russian prison. They said they were sorry, gave her a good reference, a pay check for three months, and wished her good luck in finding a new job. Then she understood everything more clearly and realized she worked for an agency where she had to accommodate men who were spying for the Americans. The Russians now wanted my sister to spy for them after she returned to her old job.

They asked her to find out names and telephone numbers of the people who stayed in that house. My sister felt so uncomfortable when she returned. It was amazing that both the Americans and the Russians knew everything that was going on in West Germany or when my sister was in East Germany. For that reason my sister's employer had to let my sister go.

Later I will tell you that the Russians arrested my mother, asking her to find my sister because they did not know to where she disappeared. My mother went through a hard time, but later was fortunate to flee from East Berlin to West Berlin after she was tortured. This was much later, when communism made life for everyone, not only for her, unbearable. If you did not join the communist party and did not live by their rules, your life was in danger. Many people disappeared suddenly, and everybody lived in fear. The communist police were almost more violent then the Russians themselves. I was really relieved to be back in West Germany at a nice job.

A New Job for My Sister and for Me

When my sister found a very nice job as a maid in a castle which was too far from my working place, she looked and found a new job for me near her. I was sad when I resigned and had to say good-bye to the family I had come to love very much. My new job was working as a maid for everything. It was a small garden-restaurant in Scharrenberg in Bergisch Gladbach. I had to work hard and long hours in the kitchen and housecleaning and every afternoon for three to four hours serving guests. I was not really happy there and missed my previous job very much. The only thing what kept me there was I was close to my sister.

It was on a Wednesday afternoon when my sister had a free day and asked me if I would come to the castle because she was all by herself in that beautiful castle, her employers were all gone. I went there and we had so much fun together playing and dressing up like princesses. Then my sister found in the newspaper in the classified section an ad asking for two young girls to share their free time with two young boys, mostly for sport events. It was mentioned that they owned a car and a yacht. We were so exited and answered with a poem we created.

Both of us are really gifted in writing poems. We had so much fun doing this, and in the poem we wrote about two very young girls, not bad looking, loving sport activities, who can't wait to meet them and are looking forward to spending free times driving with them by car or yacht in a world of adventures and happiness. I can't really explain this comical poem in English, but it was written in a funny and unique way.

Days went by without us hearing anything from them. We waited every day, anxious for an answer. We waited almost three weeks before a letter arrived. It was from an older man who put in an ad asking for a mature woman to do housekeeping and cooking. When he received the poem from us, he did not understand what it really meant. It was a puzzle for him why two young girls answered with a poem. He asked us in his letter if we could meet, and we did. We met for coffee and talked all about his ad and why we answered him with that poem. We had to laugh when we found out the mix-up in the address on the envelope. His ad was right underneath the ad from the boys, and we mixed up the addresses. That is why the mail went to him.

We discussed all kinds of possibilities to work for him and to move in with him in his house in Bad Godesberg.

It was a good thing that this mix-up happened, because it turned out that all three of us were happy with the decision we made. He owned a nice house with several rooms and was so happy when we moved in with him and that he wouldn't be so lonely anymore. My sister and I did the housekeeping and managed the cooking, and he showed us so much thankfulness and treated us with so much appreciation. Our relationship got closer, and he became our "Uncle Toni." He changed one room for my sister (who studied art in Dresden before she escaped) to an atelier, where she could paint in her free time. We were happy there for approximately two years, when suddenly a scholarship for studying at the University in Muenster/Westfalen was offered to my sister. This was her goal anyway, so she excepted this offer and moved to Muenster in Westfalen. There she met her husband and got married.

I did not hear from her after that, but I knew she immigrated with her husband and two sons to Canada. It was thirty years later when I met her in Canada.

For me it was not the same anymore without my sister. I did not feel comfortable and fulfilled living all by myself with Uncle Toni in that big house. But what could I do? I did not want to disappoint and leave him. I was sixteen years old and wanted to change this situation but was not brave enough to tell him.

Destiny Clicked in and the Lord Took Over and Decided the Next Step

I did not pray for a long time and took everything for granted, but one day when I was brought to the hospital to have my appendix removed I met a woman lying in the bed beside me who was for sure sent by the Lord. Our conversation was all about God. We became close friends, and when she was released from the hospital she left her address behind.

After I was discharged I contacted her right away and found out she was living in a Deacon Home as a deaconess. I did visit her, and at that moment I knew this was a sign from the Lord. I decided to become a deaconess and moved to Bad Kreuznach/Rheinland.

The Lord touched my heart when I heard all these beautiful deaconesses worshipping the Lord Jesus Christ. I felt so holy and heard God's voice whispering in my ear, "I love you." I knew then that He had never left me and was all the time with me by my side. I wanted to give my life to Jesus Christ and to live only for Him.

How exited I was! I could not sleep thinking about how my life would change after I became a deaconess living this kind of life.

After I had to work in a children hospital and with children with mental illnesses and learned to serve the Lord by helping others, the dedication date to give my heart to the Lord was set in ten weeks. I got my deaconess uniform, where I had to sew in my name. For Sundays and holidays or other special occasions we had a black uniform and for work a blue and sometimes dark grey. The aprons were white or blue. The caps were all white but had different shapes for the special rank of the deacon's sister's status.

In the evening before I went to bed I tried on the uniform and posed before the mirror to find myself pretty in that uniform. I always took much care of my appearance and was maybe sometimes a little bit too proud, but my heart was soft and compassionate for people who needed help.

Eight weeks before the consecration was scheduled, I was asked to take a four week holiday to see my family for the last time in the next five years. I was really excited to share all the good things happening to me with my family. It seemed to me that things in East Germany were not so bad anymore, and because nothing had happened to me the last time I was home on holiday, I decided to go to East Germany to see my family without any fear.

Seeing My Family in East Germany Again

Again I traveled to East-Germany, thinking everything over there has changed for the better. I could not be happier; my heart was overwhelmed with joy.

On the way, whenever the train stopped at a train station, all I could see were Russian soldiers with rifles on their shoulders. They did not look friendly when they checked every passenger who was on this train. To step out to stretch the legs when there was a stop was not allowed. They took the passports away and brought them back after they were inspected. In the passport, which everyone had to carry with them all the time were names, addresses, and where they had lived and worked for the last three years. I felt a big difference between the East and the West, even if it was one country. My passport must have been in order, and after they questioned me about why I came to East Germany and I told them to visit my family, they believed me and gave me my passport back.

When I got home we hugged each other over and over and cried for happiness. My older sister was the only one not home, but I heard she was studying art in Muenster/Westfalen and had married.

I was very happy to be home and enjoyed every day.

Two weeks went by and I almost forgot that my holiday would soon be over and I would have to leave, going back to the life I had chosen to become a deaconess. I could not even buy things I was used to buying in West Germany. I had such a good time that this was not a big issue for me. In every store windows you could see only empty boxes, and in the stores all the shelves were empty and were filled with boxes without anything in them. Everything was so strange for me, because sometimes you could see a long line of people before a store. Everyone who passed by that store was automatically joining the crowd and put themselves at the end of that line, not knowing what could be on sale that day. You bought it anyway, because it could take a long time until some food or other stuff was delivered to one of the stores in our village. No matter what it was, you took advantage of this rare opportunity and bought it. I had totally forgotten how it was when I left my home some years ago and what a drastic difference there was between West Germany (where the Americans took over) and East Germany (where the Russians took over). Sometimes you forget some of these hardships when everything works out fine for you, after you successfully escaped from the Russian Zone.

Meeting My Husband and Staying in East Germany

Still being a teenager and enjoying having fun, I went with my girlfriend on a Saturday night to a disco. We had so much fun on the dance floor. For me it was so new being with other young people my age or only a little older. A young man in a white and blue sailor's uniform came across the dance floor asking me for a dance. My face turned red and I could hardly talk. He was darkly tanned and looked so handsome in that pretty uniform. For me it was so surprising that he chose me out of all the other girls.

He fell in love with me and we got closer and closer. When he heard I had to go back to West Germany to become a deaconess, he was so sad and begged me not to go and to stay with him. Since I was in love too, I decided to stay in East Germany despite the unfortunate living situations. It was a sudden decision, but when you are in love for the first time, you do not need long to question your decision.

One day the communist party asked him to run a youth hostel in Oberwiesenthal, which is not far from my home village, Cranzahl. He needed a partner with whom to manage the sixty-person youth hostel, so he asked me to marry him and take this job together.

I said yes to that marriage proposal even though both of us were very young.

Everything went fine for us because, as youth hostel managers, we got lots of privileges and did not lack food at all, but we were not really happy.

When our first child (a daughter) arrived, my husband had to join the SED (Sozialistische Einheitspartei Deutschland) Party. They told us that to be a leader for the youth you have to be a member of communism. They expected me to join the FDJ (Freie Deutsche Jugend) and to lead a youth group for young people age fourteen to seventeen years old. They wanted us to be more and more involved in communist events.

When I led the FDJ group we did lots of fun stuff, but they found out I never talked about political things. I was watched very closely, so I had to be careful. It made me really frustrated.

My husband had to attend many SED conferences and party lessons that most of the time took place in other cities where he had to stay, often for a whole week. He was not often home and therefore we didn't see each other on a regularly basis, which made my life with a little baby very difficult.

I had all these responsibilities and duties in that youth hostel to run it by myself with a little baby not even one year old. I had a maid for some housekeeping and to help in the kitchen, but to cook for sometimes sixty people was, for such a young girl like me, not easy. I was without my husband, often for longer than a month, by myself with all the problems which occurred day by day. When he was home we argued about these things all the time but could not find a way out. Our marriage was anything but happy. Often we discussed how good it would be if we were free and not always separated. The relationship between us was not peaceful anymore, and our little girl did not see her father regularly, that often made me angry.

One day I got seriously sick and had to go in a hospital for an operation. I was told to stay in the hospital for at least two weeks or longer. My husband made the decision to take our little girl to an aunt living in Wolfsburg, in West Germany, to babysit her. You need a really good reason to get permission to leave East Germany and to travel to West Germany. It was not hard for my husband to get one because he had a good reason, and most of all he was known for being active as a good communist.

Husband and Baby Escaping to West Germany While I Am in the Hospital (1953)

When my husband visited me, he told me his plan not to come back. He said this was the best time to have a convincing reason to bring our little nine-month-old daughter to an aunt in West Germany to take care of her until I am healthy again. He thought it would not be a serious problem for me, once I was released from the hospital, to be reunited with my husband and child, wherever they were. He also asked me not to say a word about knowing that staying in West Germany for good was his plan.

Two weeks later I was released from the hospital and my husband's permit to stay in West Germany expired. Still in recovery, I was living with my parents-in-law in their home without hearing anything from my husband or his aunt. I could not sleep and was so restless because I had to carry this big secret with me. I did not tell anyone. We also had no contact with his aunt at all; there were no telephones.

After two more weeks, one morning a police officer showed up informing me I had to go the next day at a certain time to the Russian Headquarters in Annaberg. I was so nervous, because I assumed they knew by now my husband was not coming back. I was questioned for hours. I think they did not believe me when I told them I did not know anything about his plan and that he never discussed such a thing with me. They did let me go, but I was restricted to staying within 50 kilometers of the city where I lived. They watched me day and night like a hawk. Wherever I went, even shopping in town, I saw a person watching me.

I was living with the fear of not seeing my girl again. I missed her so much, but I believed she was in good hands. These thoughts lightened my sadness, and my prayers were with her every day.

The youth hostel was closed for a while, but later a new manager was selected by the SED Party.

Since we did not hear anything from my husband or his aunt, we started to be concerned. My father-in-law was very angry with his only son and could not understand how he could not even care about his wife (me). I could not tell him what I knew, because he was a very convinced communist and he would never understand his son leaving East Germany. He thought something terrible must have happened to his son.

My life changed drastically, because all the privileges we had as youth hostel managers were gone.

The village, Cranzahl, where I lived with my family before I moved to Oberwiesenthal with my new husband, was located in the fifty km zone I was allowed to travel. For a long, long time I had no contact with my mother. When I tried to visit her, I could not believe what had happened in the meantime. I did not even know what my mother had gone through in the last months. She was held and tortured by the Russian Commander and questioned about my sister, even she did not know anything about her.

The good news is that my mother, with my little sister, successfully escaped from East Berlin to West Germany by airplane with a help of a dear friend of hers who lived in East Berlin, which gave me so much relief. I felt guilty not staying in touch with my mother and having so much to deal with my personal life, but for her to be free, that was all that mattered.

My oldest brother was the only one of my family who stayed in Cranzahl, my hometown. He got a master degree as a tailor and opened his own shop. He was not bothered in any way by the police. My younger brother had managed to flee to West Germany some time earlier. I don't know any details about his escape, but later he immigrated to Canada too.

Left alone with my problems, at least I was in some way relieved that my family (except my older brother with his family) managed to flee to West Germany to be free.

I went sadly back to my parents-in-laws. They all blamed me for the things that happened, which maybe changed my husband's mind about the communist world. I was not even able to talk with my father-in-law, he was so angry toward me, and my mother-in-law was sad and very quiet. My sister-in-law understood most of it and was on my side, but I did not confide in her that my husband did plan this escape for a long time. My heart was troubled, I had no idea what tomorrow would bring.

I remember praying to the only source I knew who could bring help. O God, what should I do, and how long will I be separated from my little baby girl? I missed her so much and I knew she missed her mother, too. What could it be that I didn't hear anything from my husband? The situation I was in is indescribable. My wounds were not even healed and I felt so sick to my stomach. *O Lord, please help me!*

Telegram: Husband's Fatal Accident

One morning the doorbell rang and a telegram for me from my husband's aunt was handed to me. It said: "Your husband was killed in a car accident, Funeral held on [date] in Wolfsburg. Please come!"

I was shocked and did not know if this was the truth or a way to get me there to be united with him and my baby. My sister-in-law could not stop crying. We all were smitten by this news, and even though I thought this was a last attempt for my husband to get me over to West Germany, I could not exclude the thought that this might be true.

My mother and father-in-law had a hard time getting over the loss of their only son, and so did my sister-in-law.

They did not doubt at all that my husband was really killed in a car accident. Finally I thought like them and we all mourned. We discussed all kinds of possibilities if we should attend the funeral. My father-in-law, my sister-in-law, and I decided to apply for a permission to travel to Wolfsburg in West Germany to be there to pay our respect. I could not help myself, still hoping this telegram was false and a last try by my husband to get me out of here.

We were accommodated by the police to travel to the Russian Headquarters in Annaberg to apply for a travel-permit to Wolfsburg in West Germany to attend my husband's funeral.

We all were dressed in black when we applied, and on our faces they could see how sad we were. Our eyes were red from crying, and since my father-in-law was a respected and honorable communist, the authority at the headquarters did not doubt this incident. We showed the telegram to them and they believed us and gave the permission to the three of us for a certain time, to be back in eight days.

We made arrangements for traveling the next day. I remember how much trouble my sister-in-law and I went through to get black nylons. In those days all women wore dresses. Only for skiing or other kinds of sports would women wear pants. How happy we were when we finally each got a pair of black nylons.

I would like to mention that skiing in Oberwiesenthal, where the Olympic Winter Competition took place, was the most active sport besides ice hockey. You find great mountains there, and the mountain Fichtelberg was the one where all these activities took place. My husband often got prizes for winning the first or second place in Langlauf (cross-country) skiing.

The Youth Hostel was built on the top of a big hill, and to get in town we had to use the skies. It was fun for me, and sometimes I took my little baby girl in a special backpack and skied down the hill for shopping or doctor appointments. Oberwiesenthal is a beautiful place surrounded by forest and mountains.

Back to our journey to travel to West Germany to attend my husband's funeral. When we were sitting across from each other in the train, we hardly spoke, and the sadness in my father-in-law's eyes really got to me. I did hold the hands of my sister-in-law, and we looked in each other eyes with a little bit of hope that my husband did fake his accident.

When the train stopped for a while in Leipzig I got out to stretch my legs and to be with my thoughts by myself. A lady who lived in Oberwiesenthal saw me and asked, "Who died, because you're dressed in black?" When I told her we were on the way to my husband's funeral in Wolfsburg where he was killed in a car accident, she looked at me like she had seen a ghost and said: "That can't be. I saw your husband with my own eyes standing at the train station in Wolfsburg wearing a white trench coat. He told me he is waiting for you!"

My heart was pounding. Was it really true? Tears of joy came in my eyes, and I asked her again and again, "Did you really see my husband with your own eyes?"

I was so shocked, my brain could not function when my sister-in-law stepped out wondering what was going on. When she heard her brother was alive and well, she too was overwhelmed and tears of joy ran down her face.

Both of us were afraid to tell our father what we had heard, that his son was seen alive at the train station in Wolfsburg and that he told the woman who lived in our city, Oberwiesenthal, he was waiting for his wife to arrive. We went back to our seats, staring at each other and saying not one word. We thought, *He will see it for himself when we are there.*

When the train stopped at the station in Wolfsburg, I got out first, running into my husband's arms. Yes, he was wearing a white trench coat. When he saw me, I remember him saying, "You look good dressed in black." My sister-in-law got out next, hugged my husband, and told him how happy she was to find him alive. But when my father-in-law saw my husband standing there smiling at us, he got very angry, slapped him on his face, and told him he had no son anymore, that he was dead for him.

There was no doubt in my husband's mind that everybody at home assumed the telegram was a hoax, and for him the only trick was to get his wife safely to West Germany. I was so happy and could not wait to see my little baby. We all went to my aunt's home, where I finally took my girl in my arms and did not want to let her go. She was holding me so tight, I realized how much she must have missed me.

We all were a happy family, except my father-in-law. He did not talk to anybody and went home with his daughter, not even saying good-bye to one of us. It was terrible to see father and son in such a hostile situation.

In the meanwhile, a devastating tragedy happened at home with my mother-in-law. She committed suicide by drowning in a nearby lake. She told friends she could not get over the loss of her beloved only son. This sad misfortune and disaster brought lots of mourning to each of us, and it took a long time to get over it. My father-in-law did not forget or forgive his son, as long as he lived, they never talked to each other again. This tragedy brought a total split between them.

My husband and I had to face a big struggle to live a decent life. We could not stay at our aunt's small home and had to look for our own place. Life got really though, because in those days no homes were available. Your name was put on a waiting list until your turn came. My husband found a job in VW-Werk (Volkswagen factory), where he had to work so hard for a minimum wage. It was so devastating for me that we could not find a place where all three of us could stay together. We found a family who gave us a room in their house, but they did not allow kids. I cannot even find words to explain what we went through. We found a single mother in the next city (Celle) who would take care of our daughter for not too much pay, so I could work and contribute to the living expenses. We were not happy at all, but this was the life we had to manage. I worked as a waitress, mostly late and night shifts. The pay was not good and my attention was focused on being very friendly and getting good tips. My mind was always with my baby, but we could not find any solution to the situation. On a free day I visited my girl unannounced and found her lying in a crib crying. I could not believe my eyes, how she suffered and how she looked. When I changed her diapers and saw how her bottom was infected and the rash all over her back, I was heartbroken. She was holding me so tight and did not take her arms away from me. *What should I do? I can't let her stay here!* I put her in my car and took her with me.

Arriving at our room, our landlord did not want her to stay with us. He gave us one night. The next day, after my husband went to work, I took my little girl, went to the Municipal Registration Office, put my girl on the officer's desk, and told them I would not leave this office until they provided housing for us. I was stubborn and did not leave; I had to be strong for my daughter. They made many phone calls, because they did not know what to do either. I stayed the whole night in a room right beside the office, and my girl was comforted with food and a blanket from compassioned staff. It was not really a peaceful night, but I did not let my daughter out of my arms and we were finally together.

This action worked! The next morning the supervisor and his assistant showed up and we got their attention. I showed them my daughter's bottom and they understood my frustration.

They realized the serious emergency and provided two-bedroom housing for us in a wood barrack with a table, chairs, two beds, and a stove in it. My husband was so relieved and happy. We even brought attention to our financial situation and got governmental help with the rent.

I was able to change this cold environment into a cozy home. I prayed with thankfulness for the Lord's help.

We lived there for almost two years when I got pregnant again. It was not really planned, but it happened. We felt our world was too crushed to feed another child and provide for their future, but a beautiful and healthy little baby boy was born. Where there is room for three, there will be room for four, right? Yes, we thought so, but we were looking for a bigger place close to the VW factory where my husband worked, and we found a beautiful three-bedroom home in Wolfsburg. My husband worked a lot of overtime, which helped us to buy some furniture.

Our marriage was not as happy as it should be. I was home all day to take care of the kids (three and one year old) while my husband was much involved in sports and went almost every weekend skiing to Bad Harzburg. I could not go with him because I had no babysitter.

The time we were together we argued, and we finally decided to get a divorce. That was another hardship for the children. My mother, who had escaped earlier to West Germany, was living in Hiltrup/Westfalen and took care of both children after the divorce. I am still so thankful for that. After the divorce my husband and I stayed friends and everything went fine with visiting our children, who had a nice home with my mother. I moved to Wolfenbuettel/Niedersachsen and attended a business school, where I upgraded my education and learned how to become a secretary. In my free time, almost every weekend, I visited my children.

The friendship between my husband and I was suddenly over after he re-married and I got married again. He did not want any relationship with me or my mother anymore, and one day he took both kids with him. Big fights about the children took place, and both children were put in an institution. I went through so much heartache, but finally both children were released to me and lived together with me and my new husband in harmony.

After my education as a secretary was completed, I got a good job as a steno-typist for a road and bridge construction company. I was happy with my life.

The children grew up, and as a teenager my daughter moved to another city to become a cosmetologist and worked in a beauty salon.

She married very young and lived her own life independently.

My boy found a place in Ostfriesland in an educational institution, where he finished his school and became an apprentice as a bookbinder. He lived with boys his age in that reformatory home. Later he moved in with his girlfriend and her family and seemed to be very happy there. This relationship turned out later in a marriage. I really was relieved that both children became so successful and such strong, independent people.

I was married for seven years when my husband died suddenly of a heart attack when he was at work driving a business van.

At this time I got a very promising job offer in Bonn-Bad Godesberg, working in a Bundesamt for the government. I remembered Uncle Toni, where I lived with my sister, and I moved in with him for a short time until I met the young man who later became my husband. This job brought me lots of success. I made my way up from a steno-typist to a secretary and later a competent official with my own department, Civic Protection. I thought this is so amazing. My financial state would finally be secure, and maybe my dream to one day have my own house would come true.

After one year of marriage we decided to visit my sisters and one brother who had immigrated many years ago to Alberta, Canada. My sisters lived in Edmonton and my brother in High Prairie, north of Edmonton. It was an exciting holiday and we fell in love with this beautiful land, the amazing Rocky Mountains, and how people live here. They don't take every little detail so seriously in life like Germans do. Here in Canada the most important priority is family life and outside activities. I was really impressed by the free lifestyle but not totally convinced I could live here for good. My husband, though, did love everything there, and together with my younger sister they tried to persuade me to move there too. I was not sure if I could be happy here.

My little sister, who was not so little anymore, was married with three children. She would love to have me close to her and she talked to my husband about all the possibilities this land had for my husband's trade as an experienced and specialized bricklayer. For me it was not even an option, because I loved my job in Germany and did not want to start a new life in a country I didn't know and where I didn't know the language.

We enjoyed camping in the Rockies and this holiday, which let us forget for a short time how stressful life was in Germany. For me it was an unforgettable adventure, and most of all it brought me happiness to meet my siblings again after so many years.

Back in Germany, life went on like usual. I was happy, but my husband still talked enthusiastically about Canada. After six month we got a letter from Immigration Centre wherein they ask us if we were still interested in immigrating to Canada, because a job offer for my husband as a bricklayer had arrived from a company in Edmonton, Alberta. They offered him a good salary of eighteen dollars an hour for the first three months and later a raise. That was huge in 1980. We did not really know how this came about, because we did not apply for that. We found out that my sister had gone to this company and asked them if they could send that job offer; she knew they were desperately looking for experienced workers.

We were asked to come in for an interview. My husband was so excited, and for me this incident opened a very new perspective. The discussion between my husband and I went on, and he reminded me how much I would like to own a house with property, which would take many years of saving in Germany.

With this good salary we would be able to manage a mortgage and buy a house. In Canada the property in buying a house is always included, which is different from Germany, where the cost of the property is higher than the house itself. Even to find a property was almost impossible for middle-class people.

All these possibilities occupied my mind, and we made an appointment with the immigration officer. After the interview they started to prepare the paperwork, and it did not take long when we got the confirmation to immigrate to Edmonton in Canada. For me there was no going back, and I had to give notice of my three month contract of leaving. I had still some holiday open, and I took it and was busy with preparations, taking out all the savings, which was a little bit over ten thousand dollars, and sending it to my sister to make a down payment on a house near hers. Everything went so fast, and the house my sister bought for us was a bi-level because my mother who lived all by herself in Wolfenbuettel moved with us to Canada. A pensioner who has family living in Canada has no problem immigrating. When we arrived on April 4, 1980, at the airport in Edmonton, my sister drove us right away to our new house. It was a very nice looking house with two bedrooms and a washroom on the upper level; the kitchen and living room on the main floor; a livingroom, a bedroom and a washroom on the middle level; and a big basement ready to build a recreation area. We could not withhold our joy.

Dreaming of a New Life in Canada

What could go wrong now? We thought everything was under control and all we had to do was be thankful. My husband worked only three weeks when they went on strike, which we did not know is, in Canada, a normal situation. That brought us some headache, because we depended on my husband's income to be able to pay the mortgage. We called my brother in High Prairie and told him about our frustration. He offered my husband a small job helping him build an addition on his little house. He was not able to pay big bucks, but at least it was a small pay and free food.

It was June 4, 1980, exactly two months after we immigrated, when we drove with our second-hand car to High Prairie.

The weather was not good, and the closer we came to my brother's place the more it was raining. When we arrived in High Prairie it was already getting dark. We phoned my brother and asked him to pick us up in town. He lived nine miles from town, and to get there you had to know the place, and the road condition in the rain was like driving through soap. We had no idea how dangerous it is to drive on a gravel road in those weather conditions.

What about Our Dream We Had?

The dream and the joy of starting a new life in Canada crashed totally after the car accident two months after we immigrated.

Our life changed drastically when our brother picked us up and drove before us to his place.

He knew the road very well, and we saw his back light when we followed him. Suddenly we did not see his back lights anymore and my husband sped up a little bit, scared we would lose him. I was nervous and afraid and was not acting calm toward my husband as I should have. My husband lost control of the car which landed upside down in a ditch filled with water where I was found while my husband was not seen anywhere.

After my brother came back to see why we did not followed him, he was devastated to see what had happened to us. The car was totally smashed. I was sitting in the water screaming with pain because my pelvis was fractured on both sides.

My brother phoned for help, and when his friend and the ambulance arrived they could not find my husband. He was almost twenty meters away, thrown in the field, and they had to search for him. When they found him and brought him to the hospital, right away they flew him to the University Hospital in Edmonton. I did not understand at all what had happened to my husband because I had to deal with my own pain.

I was treated in the town hospital of High Prairie, and when they touched me to cut off my clothes, I was screaming in pain. In one way I was a little bit mad that I did not hear any screaming from my husband, who I felt was responsible for the car accident. I did not know they had flown him to Edmonton and assumed he would be dead by now. Not one person was telling me anything about him; I was kept in the dark, which made me even more angry. I did not understand the English language, and my brother who could translate was not with me.

I experienced lots of problems because of the lack of the language. Later I found out why my brother could not be with me. He was with my husband in Edmonton, and together with my caring sister they stayed with my husband, who did not come out of a coma. The doctors and nurses gave up on him and had no hope that he would ever come out, but if he did, he would be a vegetable all his life. When I asked my brother if he could let my husband speak on a tape so I could hear his voice, I heard from him all these terrible things that had happened to my husband. I was so thankful to my brother and younger sister that they stayed day and night with him. I knew they waited for any changes in his condition to bring me good news.

Weeks went by, but my husband was still in a coma.

I started praying again, and I was sure only prayers could bring miracles. I asked my brother if I could speak on a tape and they could let my husband hear my voice. We did, and I spoke all the lovely words which would make him happy. I said how I loved him and couldn't wait to be with him in harmony without any of the anger I had in the car toward him. A head phone was put on my husband's head and they played my messages.

Did I tell you that prayers are powerful and brings miracle? Suddenly they saw a tear running down his face when he heard me speaking to him, and they realized he was alive and could hear. All my relatives prayed continually. The doctor saw on the x-ray that he might have a broken neck. They started to put some nails in his left and right forehead and made preparations behind his bed to put him on that.

Many readers will doubt what happened, but it is the truth. My brother prayed in the Holy Spirit in agreement with my sister that my husband would fully recover and not have a broken neck. I was not there, but I heard afterward that my brother was, after his prayers, so weak he had to be accompanied by my sister to the waiting room because he was too weak to walk by himself.

The miracle happened. They made another x-ray before they put my husband on that stand behind his bed, and they could not believe what they saw—*no broken neck!* Many of you will say there was never such a thing, but we knew it was the miracle of prayer. In front of his bed a television was installed and a picture of me was put on the left upper corner. Very often he opened his eyes a little bit and stared in that direction where my photo was put.

My broken hips made good recoveries, and the doctors agreed to transfer me to the Misericordia-Hospital in Edmonton. I was happy but still not able to be released, and I begged the doctors to let me visit my husband in the nearby University Hospital. They thought it was too early but agreed to allow my sister to transport me in her car with a wheelchair to my husband.

This was the turning point, when my husband realized I was there. He opened his eyes more and more and even tried to form a word. His face and his left side were totally paralyzed. Not one of the doctors had hope with this severe brain damage that he would ever function normally, if he even recovered.

One day my husband opened his eyes and saw me sitting beside his bed. His face was so deformed. He was staring at me and looked really scary, and fears came over me. I thought that could not be my husband because he looked like a totally different person. Maybe what scared me off were the many tubes and the machines he was hooked on.

He tried to let us know that he wanted me to bend over to him, but it was impossible for me. I was still in the wheelchair and not able to get up without pain, and the doctor instructed my sister to make sure to follow his instructions because of the healing process of my broken pelvises. On my left pelvis was a complicated fracture.

At that time we did not even know if he could understand what we were saying to him, because we could not see any reaction. Doctors and nurses tried to prepare us that he would never be normal with such severe brain damage.

My sister was always with my husband and stayed every day by my husband's bed. Before she went to bed she phoned the nursing station to ask for any new developments. Three times a week she picked me up from the other hospital in my wheelchair and I spent a whole day at his bedside in the hospital. I will never be able to repay my little sister for what she did for both of us.

Days went by and we saw frustration in the eyes of my husband. He could not move, only stare at me. I felt he must be in pain and wanted us to know something. My sister and I looked at his mouth because he tried to tell us something. We asked him so many times if he meant this or that. We felt how angry and frustrated he must feel, because a no was when he closed his eyes for a moment.

The days I could not be with him there was no improvement at all. After I was released I went on crutches; my sister took me to him every single day. While I was sitting by his bed he heard me praying, and what a wonder, I saw his effort to bring his right hand to where he could move four fingers to his other hand; it showed me he wanted to pray with me. I could not stop crying and everyone who came in that room cried with me. Many hospital visitors stopped at my husband's room to see if there was news about my husband, and some of them prayed with me.

I felt so much hope, and my faith was increasing that this could be possible. Every day I put my hand over my husband's hand and we prayed in unity, even I was not totally sure if he understood. But in the Holy Spirit I was sure. There was a pastor in the hospital who visited the patients regularly. When my husband was in a condition to let others know what he wanted, he was asking for this pastor to come on his bed and speak blessings over our marriage. This was really a big surprise for me since we weren't married in a church and my husband never had the desire. He held my hand so tightly and tears ran over his face. The presence of the Lord was there.

I could go on writing about what I went through with my husband's attitude change, but my faith in miracles never left me.

Remember, we came to Canada in April 1980, without knowledge of the language. In June 1980, exactly two month later: the accident happened. Our life seemed to be over. How could we manage if my husband was paralyzed and disabled and I was physically unable to work? For me to get a job in an office, where I could sit, I had to first go to school to learn the English language.

Two month later, in October 1980, my husband was transferred from the University of Alberta Hospital to the Glenrose Hospital Rehabilitation Centre. The nurses and physiotherapists did such a good job, and we saw more and more improvement. For me everything was a little easier since I did not have to be with my husband every day.

My mind was set to go to school and study this foreign language. My sister (I was still on crutches) went with me to the Grant McEwan Collage for registration and testing. Every student had to sit at a desk by themselves. My sister was only allowed to sit beside me because I was on crutches.

I was so nervous when every student was handed a six pages questionnaire. I looked over it and started to freak out. I could not understand one question. My sister was not allowed to talk to me or even make any gestures. I marked every question but did not know what I was doing.

After two hours the teacher collected the tests, and after a one-hour recess every student got the results of which of the five levels for English as a Second Language they were put.

When the teacher came to my desk she asked if she could talk to my sister. What do you think she said? She could not even understand why my sister had brought me to this college without a clue or any basic grasp of this language. I had none of the questions answered correctly. She suggested I had to go first to an ABC Course for ESL. My sister was more disappointed than me because she thought I was so smart I could learn anything I set my mind on. Usually I can, but this is something you have to have some knowledge of.

The next day my sister went to the teacher again and begged her to give me a chance because I had to learn fast to make a living, since my husband was paralyzed and in a wheelchair and would never be able to work in his life and needed 24/7 care. She told her how smart I was and what a fast learner I was. I was touched that she thought so highly of me.

The teachers came together to discuss my situation, and they felt sorry for me. They agreed to put me in a separate room to listen to tapes and study all by myself. I was anxious and willing to study as hard as possible. My days were so hard, and when I came home I had to take care of my husband, who could not walk by himself and was sitting in the wheelchair the whole day. He managed to go on a special toilet stool. His mouth was pulled to one side, which made it very difficult to feed him. When he ate by himself it was a mess. Cleaning and taking care of all that, on top of lots of homework, made my daily life terrifying. I had only a few hours sleep and always the disturbance of my husband, who could not understand why I was not there for him during the day, always going out of the house and doing homework till midnight; that was so frustrating for him. He turned violent sometimes, which often frightened me and sometimes my mother, who was not so young anymore and tried to stay during the day in her suite or with my sister.

I put myself in his shoes to understand what he must be going through. I told myself over and over I had to be strong; there was no other way. *There will be a tomorrow for us. Keep going. The sun is shining for everyone.*

After I studied all by myself for about three weeks in a classroom, I was tested about my English. I passed the test and could join Level 1. I was so proud of myself and knew only my prayers and the help of God had brought me through this hard time. I enjoyed studying more and more at that great Grant McEwan Collage. The joy and excitement of being a student with great marks and passing each level brought happiness to my life. At home my husband was more and more able to feed himself and to take care of himself while he was in the wheelchair. Every morning he was picked up by D.A.D's Ambulance for physiotherapy, which gave me more peace and time to study. I finished four levels with success and graduated after eighteen month.

Now I started looking for a job but found only a part-time job at the other end of town. I worked in a office for six-dollar an hour, which did not help me much, and the travel expenses were so high I had to quit.

Our financial situation was no longer bearable. My husband and I felt this was too much to handle and we seriously discussed ending our lives. I remember when we looked in each other eyes figuring out how to do it. We were crying and did not let anybody know what our plan was. The only easy way for us to commit suicide was to take a overdose of sleeping pills, but where would we get such a big amount of sleeping pills? We also were afraid that maybe one of us would survive, and what about the survivor? We went through sleepless nights and found no solution. We talked about how this would affect my children in Germany, my mother and siblings here in Canada, and the parents of my husband, who did not want us from the beginning to move to Canada. All these thoughts made us realize we couldn't do it.

The only way to survive was by selling our house. I contacted the real estate office and they put a sale sign in front of our house.

One afternoon my husband had a stroke and was brought to the hospital. Without any money it was hard for me to afford visiting him in the hospital downtown. I thought how much worse my life could get. My husband's doctor told me I should take the sale sign away and tell my husband about it, because he thought this was the main reason for his stroke. I asked the real estate office to put a hold on the sale and take the sign off our property. When I told this to my husband I saw how relieved he was, because to own this house he loved so much was his big dream. The paralysis on the left side of his face got normal again, and after two weeks he was discharged. When we got home he was so happy not to see that sale sign on our house.

But our situation did not change, so I had to convince him that selling the house was our only chance. It took a lot of wisdom to convince him. The sign was put back, but the market for selling houses was so bad, no buyers showed up. I put an ad in a German newspaper Kanada Kurier, saying "House by owner for sale. Must sell for personal reason." We got some answers, but the offer we got was even less than the original price, and what about the mortgages we paid for three years and our down payment? It looked really bad to get a decent price or even to get our down payment back.

One day we got a phone call from the *Kanada Kurier* office asking us about our story. I told him a little bit and he felt so sorry for us. He made an appointment to meet with us. When the reporter from Winnipeg working for that magazine arrived, he put a microphone on the table before us and he interviewed us for hours. He saw my husband sitting in the wheelchair not able to speak properly. The nice reporter showed so much compassion and asked us for permission to put this story in his magazine. We agreed and he left. We did not hear from him for a long time until we saw the article about our life in the newspaper.

My health condition was falling apart, and I had a nervous breakdown and was committed to a clinic for mental care. I did not want to see or speak to anyone and liked to stay in a dark room by myself. My mother was living with my sister, and I refused to take any phone calls. My husband tried desperately to talk to me, but I refused. The doctors and nurses tried all kinds of treatments, but nothing brought me out of this darkness.

One afternoon I could not believe my eyes. My husband was standing in my room and did not leave. He worried about me so much that he took all his strength to put himself, without any other help, in the car, and he drove to the clinic. He wanted to tell me good news, but I did not believe what he was telling me. He said every day mail with money in it arrived, and he did not know what to do. He was crying and begging me to come home and be with him; he did not want to live without me anymore. He went home, and all this good news occupied my brain. After many sessions with the doctors, I felt ready to go home.

Yes, my husband was right. I found in the living room lots of letters from people who had read the article about our tragedy and sent money and comforting words. It was almost unreal how people care for each other. I gave thanks to the Lord and answered every letter. *Could this be a change in our life?*

Two unpleasant incidents did happened when help in exchange for sex was offered to me. I felt so embarrassed and insulted.

I paid all the bills which were piling up and made payments on the mortgage for some months in advance. Everything looked very promising for us, but this was a bad decision. I should never have made payments on the mortgage; rather, I should have saved the money for the time to come, moved out of our house, and moved into an apartment. We lost our home anyway since no buyer was interested in buying and the house went back to the real estate office without any reimbursement; the down payment and the payments on the mortgage for three years were gone. How stupid of me to think we could hold on to our house if there was no income and to hope I would find a good job. *What should we do now?* I contacted the government in Germany where I was employed before we immigrated and asked if I could get my job back. They gave me hope even though I would not get the same position I had before. I felt new hope for the future.

It was in January 1984 when we decided to move back to Germany. We lived at my husband's parents, but my husband was not happy at all. There were many reasons why my husband could not be happy. With his disability, he could not walk normally and sometimes was without any balance. Only his right side was managing normally. People made fun of him and thought he was drunk. Doctors suggested he would be better off in an institution for handicapped. He was really discouraged and had serious depression.

For me, I had to go on. I went to the Government Building and discussed my options to work for them again. The lady official who would become my new boss interviewed me, and a date was set when I could start. I had to go through some exam about my health condition, and the doctor told me there would be no problem. I was looking forward to the day I could start working, but my husband was so unhappy that he got more and more sick and often landed in the hospital. He did not go anywhere and stayed the whole day at home when he was not in the hospital, but I could not think of any other way to make a living.

The day came when I went early in the morning to start my new job. When I entered the room, to report to find out where my working place would be, the boss lady looked at me in surprise. She asked me if I did not get the letter where they informed me they couldn't hire me back.

I was devastated and went in my car and cried for hours.

They had three reasons they could not take me back. First, they found out that I had applied for disability pension. Second, they had to pay 10.000 DM to Interpol to investigate what I had done the last three years in a foreign country because I was a public officer working in the Secret Civic Protection Department and could have given secret information. Third, when the board had to make the last decision, all board members agreed not to hire me back after I left my homeland and could not make it in another country when they could give this job to so many unemployed people in Germany.

I was not in the position to drive home right away. For hours I sat in the car crying my eyes out. Finally I went home and told the bad news to my husband. He was excited and happy, because for him, he said, there couldn't be any better news.

I tried to get other work, but nothing was available. I got more and more discouraged and realized I could not find a job in Germany any easier than in Canada. Talking about going back to Canada before the One-Year Permit expired made my husband really happy.

But where should we live? Every one living there had no place for us and struggled with their own lives. We had to make a way before the permit to stay out of the country expired. I phoned my sister and told her how hard it had become living and working here in Germany. I was so sad, and when she heard that my husband's condition had gotten worse because he wanted to go back to Canada, she offered to let us stay in her basement, even though her basement was not made to live in.

We agreed with these living arrangements because the only thing that mattered to us was to go back to Canada before the permit expired. My parents-in-law paid for the tickets because they saw how unhappy their son was.

When we arrived at the Edmonton Airport, my husband cried for happiness. We moved into the basement and I started desperately looking for a job.

I found one! I was hired as a receptionist for evening shifts in a Shepherd's Care Centre. I loved the job, and very soon they offered me full-time work in housekeeping. I felt so blessed working full-time in housekeeping and in the evenings as a receptionist. Very soon I was asked to become a supervisor in the housekeeping department and to look after the laundry department. I felt God's mercy and His rich blessings upon us. I found a small apartment and we moved out of my sister's basement. We were so happy!

My husband's disability pension from Germany was finally approved, which was not much, but combined with my salary we were able to manage life.

We had started to feel comfortable with what we had when a phone call came from my daughter in Germany asking if we could take her two young children for a time. She was going through a very hard time and was not able to look after them. My husband and I agreed right away. We thought where there is food for two there would be food for four.

When we picked up the girls from the airport, the younger one came in the wheelchair because her knee was injured and infected. Our family doctor looked after her without any payments. He knew about our life story and showed us his great compassion. Again we knew the Lord looked after us, no matter what life brought.

A new problem arrived when we wanted the girls to attend school. I went from school to school asking if they would take the girls without paying a student fee for foreign students, which was five thousand dollars per student per year. I was lucky when the Catholic school let them study for free after all the other schools denied them. They even tried successfully to get the girls an allowance from the government, and all the books were free. It was really the Lord who opened all the doors for us. We knew He had everything under control and we gave praise to Him.

The living arrangement in a one-bedroom apartment with four people was not so comfortable for a long period of time. We found a low-rent house where the basement was big enough for the girls to sleep and have their own privacy. I worked full-time during the day and a 4-hour evening shift. My husband, who could not go anywhere by himself, stayed home and managed the cooking. The Shepherd's Care Centre where I worked was right beside a building where people over sixty could get a nice apartment. My mother lived there and I could see her every lunch break. I felt every day new blessings and miracles.

In the rented house we lived comfortably for almost two years when the girls were asked to go back to Germany because the immigration for my daughter and her children was approved, but they had to immigrate together as a whole family.

My brother, who lived all by himself after he lost his son in a car accident and afterward got divorced, sponsored for my daughter to work for him in his household. My daughter moved with her children to High Prairie, where she looked after my brother's household on a farm. The girls went to school there and lived happily together. We missed them very much since we had lived together as a family for such a long time, but knowing that they were happy was all what mattered to us.

My oldest sister (the artist) lost her husband in a car accident and was left with her five children. The husband of my younger sister died very young of a heart attack and she had to struggle with her three children. So many tragedies happened in my family. They all were believers and managed their hardships with the Lord and never gave up. It made them all stronger and more compassionate for other people who had to go through similar suffering.

My husband and I feel so blessed by how our life turned out, even dealing with my husband's mental and physical problems. His health condition is dependent on the weather or the stress he sometimes feels, but we can handle that very well because we are realizing what a great miracle happened to him that he is able to function mentally like a normal person. When because of weather conditions his face is swelling and a little bit deformed and a slight seizure occurs, he sleeps for a few hours and he is fine. Thank you, Lord!

After a while my daughter asked me if we would like to move up to High Prairie and together purchase for rent eighty acres of land which we could split and we would be closer together. Since we missed the girls so much we agreed, and many good circumstances happened to us that made the decision easy. The German disability pension I applied for came through for me along with a small amount of backpay for the time during which the application was handled. My husband's parents died and they also left us a little money. All that happened at once, which made our decision final. We made a downpayment on a mobile home and arranged setting up the place and moved in 1988 to our new home on our own land in High Prairie. With both of our disability pensions from Germany, even though they are small, we are able to live a decent life. We have learned to be content with the things the Lord gives us.

The Lord was so good to us, and we give Him day by day our thankfulness. I got my two grand-daughters baptized together with me in the Snipe Lake and we are so proud to be newborn Christians. My strong belief and faith brought me and my husband to where we are today, and the hope for tomorrow will never leave us because we know the only source for help is Jesus Christ. Life with the Lord Jesus Christ always brings hope for tomorrow!

The Berlin Wall was built in 1961 to stop East Germans from fleeing to West Germany, and the fall of Berlin was in November 1989. It will always be a symbol for the end of the Cold War. President Reagan visited Berlin in June 1987 to urge the Soviet leader, Gorbachev, to tear down the wall, but he was not successful.

After the wall came down, I visited my homeland. One evening I went to a music- and singer performance in my home dialect language.

My emotion got to me, and I could not stop crying because I was so touched hearing the girls playing and singing, reminding me so much of my childhood. They saw me crying and had trouble continuing to sing without being emotionally and contagiously connected. When they found out that I was from Canada, they wanted to talk to me after the program was over. I was really touched by their simple and content mentality that I told them to try to organize a tour for them to perform in Canada. They thought it would only be a dream because they never in over forty years had the opportunity to travel somewhere out of their little village, Crottendorf.

After I came back, I started with enthusiasm to plan for them to come to Canada and perform with their beautiful voices. Everything went so well, and everyone was excited to meet this German singer group.

I started to ask the church members of St. Paul's Lutheran Church, and they were willing to take the girls into their homes for free. Then I started organizing the flight through AMA for a good group rate. The important thing for me was to contact places where they could perform. I had no trouble at all, and many facilities wanted their entertainment and agreed to even pay and provide free food. I could not believe how anxious people were to meet people from East Germany who were finally free.

I booked so much entertainment that almost every day was booked. I also wanted them to see the Rocky Mountains, but there was one big hurdle. How and with what do we travel?

Another surprise occurred. The government from the City for Foreign Travel Department provided two six-person vans for free. We only had to pay for the gasoline. I was on cloud 9. When I

Burgel bottom left with the singing group

told the leader of this group, Crottendorfer Spatzen, she said, "This can't be true." It was even unbelievable for me. The group arrived in May 1991, and the guests' parents greeted them at the airport and took them home. Then the schedule of the performances took place.

The entertainment included Heritage Days, St. Paul's Church, the Canadian-German Culture Centre, and Millwoods Shepherds Care Centre in Edmonton.

Then we travelled to Red Deer and Calgary to perform at their Canadian-German Culture Centre. In Calgary they sang in a church, too.

We travelled to Banff, and later they sang at Lake Louise, where many people gathered and listened, overwhelmed at their folksongs in the German language. The echo from the mountains was indescribable and mysterious.

From there we drove to Jasper, and the Jasper guests' parents were contacted earlier. They welcomed them and provided accommodations for free. They performed at the Jasper Lodge, and everything went perfectly fine. I could hear their beautiful voices day and night. Wherever we went, they were singing. When we went to Radium Hot Spring, the girls sang in the pool. There was an excited atmosphere around many guests, and everyone was so friendly.

Then it was time to travel back to Edmonton, where some other performances were scheduled.

The newspaper was full with all the stories of the performances of the singing group Crottendorfer Spatzen. They sang in the radio station, where I was interviewed and asked how this all could happen, getting the East-German people out of there and here to Canada. I could make their dreams come true, which was for me a dream, too.

I was so satisfied and thankful to the Lord that I was able with HIS help, of course, to accomplish this mission for these East-German people to see for the first time the world outside their small boundary.

If you went through what they had and you have the opportunity to help, that is what the world needs. Tell yourself today to do what you can and what is in your power to help others.

Believe me, it makes you feel good and everything comes back to you in your life.

July 2009

My Present Life

I live happily with my husband on forty acres of land in our cozy mobile home in High Prairie, Alberta in February 2008 we celebrated our thirtieth wedding anniversary. We live together in harmony under the grace of God. We grew closer together and respect and appreciate each other more and more.

My daughter with the grandchildren moved to Calgary because there was a better chance for them to study at the Alberta University. They all are happy with their lives.

My son in Germany is married with two children and one grandchild. They also live a happy life, which we can see when we visit them every second year.

My mother died in my arms a few years ago. All her children and children's children were standing around her bed when the Lord took her peacefully home.

My brother married again, and my sisters in Edmonton are doing well and are happy.

God's plan for us was ready from the beginning. We were tested, tempted, and challenged in our life, but nothing separated us from the love of our Lord. Through all these tragedies we became closer to the Lord Jesus Christ.